Sunderland AFC

Richard Callaghan
MY FOOTBALL

Designed by **courage**

Text copyright © Richard Callaghan
Design copyright © **courage**

ISBN: 978 1 901888 77 5

First Published 2012

Published in Great Britain by:
My World
Chase House
Rainton Bridge Business Park
Tyne and Wear
DH4 5RA
Tel: 0191 3055165

www.myworld.co.uk

My World is an imprint of Business Education Publishers Ltd.

All rights reserved. No part of this publication, may be reproduced, stored in a retrieval system, or transmitted, in any form or by any means, electronic, mechanical, photocopying, recording or otherwise, without the prior permission of *My World*.

British Cataloguing-in-Publications Data.
A catalogue record for this book is available from the British Library.

Printed in Great Britain by Martins the Printers Ltd.

Sunderland AFC

The Foundation of Sunderland

In 1879 James Allan, a Scotsman teaching at Hendon Board School, started a football club to provide 'recreational amusement' for Sunderland's school teachers. He established the Sunderland & District Teachers Association Football Club, with the entire side being composed of teachers from the local area.

Allan was born in Ayr on October 9, 1857, and studied medicine at Glasgow University before changing career to become headmaster at Hendon Board School. Upon the club's formation he appointed himself vice captain, and still holds the record for the number of goals scored by a Sunderland player in a single game, an unbelievable twelve.

The club was based initially at Blue House Field in Hendon, close to the school where Allan taught, and played their first recorded competitive game on November 13, 1880, losing 1-0 to Ferryhill Athletic.

In 1881, when non-teachers were allowed to play for the first time the name of the club was changed accordingly, and Sunderland Association Football Club was born.

Newcastle Road
1886-1898

The home of Sunderland's great title winning sides of the 1890s, Sunderland played their games at Newcastle Road from 1886 to 1898. It was at Newcastle Road that Sunderland played the game which saw them assert their ability to play in the Football League, beating Aston Villa 7-2 in April 1890. It was also the site of the club's first game in league football, a 3-2 defeat by Burnley in September the same year. With a grandstand, a clubhouse, and a capacity of 15,000; by the time the club joined the Football League, Newcastle Road was the largest and most impressive ground in the North East. In January 1891 it recorded an attendance of 21,000, with spectators watching from the roof of the stand, for an FA Cup tie against Everton - a record in English football at the time.

Sunderland Albion

On a Tuesday night in March 1888, James Allan, the founder of Sunderland AFC, held a meeting at the Empress Hotel in Union Street. The results of that meeting would divide the town and see Allan responsible for the creation of Sunderland's first great rivals, as Sunderland Albion was born.

In an acrimonious split, Allan did not just leave Sunderland, but took seven Sunderland players with him, along with the club's first President, Alderman Potts. Allan founded Albion because he felt dissatisfied with the growing commercialism at Sunderland.

Albion played their games at Sunderland's first home, Blue House Field in Hendon and the club joined the Football Alliance, the rival to the Football League, in 1889. However Sunderland's admittance to the Football League in 1890 was a body blow to Albion's popularity.

The strength of the rivalry between the two clubs can be demonstrated by the fact that, when drawn against Albion in FA Cup and Durham Challenge Cup ties during the 1888-89 season, Sunderland chose to withdraw from the competitions rather than allow Albion to benefit from the bumper Cup crowds. Following Sunderland's title win in 1892, Albion disbanded after 4 years as Sunderland's bitterest rivals.

MANAGERS

Tom Watson
1889-1896

Taking the job in 1889, Tom Watson was Sunderland's first manager. Watson was Sunderland's most successful manager of all time, leading the club to three league titles in four seasons, 1891-92, 1892-93 and 1894-95, finishing as runners up in 1893-94. His team was known as the 'Team Of All Talents', such was their prowess on the field, and the period of success and domestic dominance which Watson masterminded was unparalleled.

Watson was just 29 years old when he took the job, building a side based on the Scottish passing game and using Scottish talent such as Jimmy Millar, Johnny Campbell, Hughie Wilson and Ned Doig, to bring joy to the Newcastle Road faithful. Watson left Sunderland in 1896, to take over at Liverpool, bringing two First Division championships to Anfield as well as taking them to their first FA Cup final in 1914. Sadly, Watson's life was cut short the following year when he succumbed to pneumonia and pleurisy, dying on May 6, 1915, aged just 56.

SUNDERLAND AFC

'A TALENTED MAN IN EVERY POSITION'
'TEAM OF ALL TALENTS'

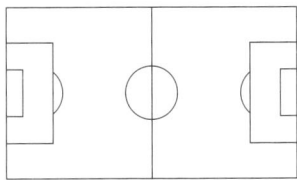

On April 5, 1890, William McGregor, the founder of the football league, gave one of the most famous quotes in Sunderland's history when he said that the club had 'a talented man in every position'. McGregor's quote came after a 7-2 demolition of his side, Aston Villa. Villa were one of the best sides in England and Sunderland's thrashing of Villa was seen as instrumental in the club's admission to the Football League the following season.

McGregor referred to Sunderland as the 'team of all talents', and it was a name that stuck. Tom Watson's formidable side were rightly regarded as one of the most dangerous teams in England during the 1890s as they stormed to three league titles before his departure for Merseyside in 1896. His side was blessed with remarkable players like Johnny Campbell, Ted Doig and Hughie Wilson, and remains one of the greatest teams ever to play in red and white.

JOHNNY CAMPBELL

154 GOALS

215 GAMES

7 YEARS (1890-1897)

Sunderland's first great centre forward, Johnny Campbell was the chief danger man of the Team Of All Talents; Campbell's record of 154 goals in 215 games makes him one of the most prolific players ever to pull on a red and white shirt. He made his debut against Blackburn Rovers on 18 January 1890, in a game Sunderland lost 4-2. He played for Sunderland for the next seven years, winning championships in 1892, 1893 and 1895, and emerging as the league's top scorer in each of these seasons.

He left Sunderland in 1897 and moved 12 miles north to play for Newcastle United, scoring 12 goals in 29 games and was instrumental in Newcastle's first promotion. Retiring from football after breaching Newcastle club rules by becoming a licensee, he remains one of Sunderland's record scorers to this day, and the type of forward we'd all love to see again.

NED DOIG

Goalkeeper
657 Games
14 Years (1890-1904)

Joining Sunderland in 1890, the 23 year old Scottish goalkeeper Ned Doig was to become one of Sunderland's longest serving players, with 14 seasons and 457 competitive appearances for the club (plus a further 200 friendly games, which if counted would make him Sunderland's highest appearance maker of all time). Doig was an eccentric character, famously so embarrassed about his baldness that he would wear a cap with a chin strap, and if the cap was blown off by the wind he would forget about the match whilst he caught it.

Doig was a central part of the famous Team of all the Talents, and his 14 years at the club saw him collect four league championships before departing to join his former manager Tom Watson at Liverpool. He played his final game for Liverpool in April 1908 at the remarkable age of 41 years and 165 days, which remains a record for the Anfield club. Doig sadly died on November 7, 1919, a victim of the Spanish Flu epidemic which swept the globe following the conclusion of the First World War.

No.1

THE 1892 TITLE

The 1891-92 season saw Sunderland claim their first title, in only their second season of league football. They finished five points clear of their closest rivals, Preston North End, winning 21 of their 26 games including all 13 games played at Newcastle Road. It was the first title for Tom Watson, the manager who would be so instrumental to Sunderland's success in the early part of the 1890s, and was due in no small part to the efforts of prolific Scottish forward Johnny Campbell, who notched 32 goals for the club that season. The club had a number of big results that season, including beating Derby 7-0 at Newcastle Road, and putting seven past Darwen both home and away.

No.2 — THE 1893 TITLE

The 1892-93 season saw Sunderland build on the previous year's success by capturing a second title in a row. Once again Preston North End were the nearest contenders, however this year the gap had widened to 11 points, due in no small part to the expansion of the Football League from 14 to 16 teams. Johnny Campbell was once again the main man, his 31 goals helping Sunderland to a league title with 22 wins and 4 draws from 30 games. These included barnstorming 6-0 and 5-0 wins against league debutants Newton Heath, a club better known by the name they adopted in 1902, Manchester United.

No.3 THE 1895 TITLE

After having missed out on a third successive title to Aston Villa in 1894, Tom Watson's Sunderland side was back with a vengeance in the 1894-95 season, topping the table with 21 wins from 30 games, and finishing 5 points ahead of nearest rivals Everton. Johnny Campbell scored 22 of the 80 goals which gave Watson his final Sunderland title, and saw Sunderland notch up a ten game unbeaten run between October 6 and December 27. Notable wins included an 8-0 victory over Derby County, 7-1 against Small Heath (later Birmingham City), while Sunderland were involved in the best attended game of the season: 35,000 witnessing a top of the table clash away at Everton which ended in a 2-2 draw.

No.2 — THE 1893 TITLE

The 1892-93 season saw Sunderland build on the previous year's success by capturing a second title in a row. Once again Preston North End were the nearest contenders, however this year the gap had widened to 11 points, due in no small part to the expansion of the Football League from 14 to 16 teams. Johnny Campbell was once again the main man, his 31 goals helping Sunderland to a league title with 22 wins and 4 draws from 30 games. These included barnstorming 6-0 and 5-0 wins against league debutants Newton Heath, a club better known by the name they adopted in 1902, Manchester United.

No.3 THE 1895 TITLE

After having missed out on a third successive title to Aston Villa in 1894, Tom Watson's Sunderland side was back with a vengeance in the 1894-95 season, topping the table with 21 wins from 30 games, and finishing 5 points ahead of nearest rivals Everton. Johnny Campbell scored 22 of the 80 goals which gave Watson his final Sunderland title, and saw Sunderland notch up a ten game unbeaten run between October 6 and December 27. Notable wins included an 8-0 victory over Derby County, 7-1 against Small Heath (later Birmingham City), while Sunderland were involved in the best attended game of the season: 35,000 witnessing a top of the table clash away at Everton which ended in a 2-2 draw.

The 1894-95 season saw Sunderland emerge as First Division champions. The team dominated the league, finishing five points ahead of nearest rivals Everton. North of the border, meanwhile, Heart of Midlothian were collecting their first ever league title, finishing five points clear of nearest rivals Celtic, and nine points clear of a third placed Rangers. Following the end of the 1894-95 season in both countries, Hearts invited Sunderland to make the journey to Edinburgh, where the two would play a match dubbed the 'Championship of the World'.

The game took place on April 27, 1895 in the Scottish capital, with the two teams contesting what must have been an entertaining fixture between two of the best sides in Britain at the time. In the end, Sunderland ran out winners, with five goals to Hearts' three, and the club was crowned the Champions of the World.

Roker Park
1898-1997

Sunderland's home for 99 years from 1898 to 1997, Roker Park was the introduction to football for generations of Sunderland fans. Opened by the Marquess of Londonderry on September 10, 1898, the event marked by a 1-0 friendly victory over Liverpool, Roker Park quickly became one of the most impressive grounds in the country.

By 1913, with the Roker end concreted, the capacity of the ground had risen to 50,000, and when the Archibald Leitch designed Main Stand was added in 1929 the capacity rose to 60,000, although some matches saw more than 75,000 crammed inside. In the end, the demands of modern football and requirements to move to all-seater stadia following the Hillsborough disaster saw Roker's capacity shrink, and the club left their old home for the last time in 1997.

MANAGERS

Alex Mackie
1899-1905

During Alex Mackie's six years in charge of Sunderland, the native of Banffshire in Scotland led Sunderland to a league title in 1902 and a win in the Sheriff of London Charity Shield against Corinthians the following year. Mackie acted as player-manager after taking over from Robert Campbell in 1899, and took charge of the club for more than 200 games, achieving a win percentage of almost 50% during his time at the reins.

After becoming embroiled in the McCombie illegal payments scandal and being suspended from football for three months, Mackie left the club, but he was not out of work long, taking over at Middlesbrough in June 1905. He left Middlesbrough in the wake of another illegal payments scandal and, disillusioned with football, he became a publican in Middlesbrough, running the Star and Garter in Marton Road.

No.4 — THE 1902 TITLE

1901-02 saw Sunderland claim their fourth league title, and their first since the departure of Tom Watson in 1896. Scotsman Alex Mackie had taken the reins in 1899, and guided Sunderland to the title, this year, 3 points ahead of Everton in second and 7 points ahead of Newcastle in third. Johnny Campbell had moved to Newcastle in 1897, so the goals came from players like Jimmy Millar, Billy Hogg and Jimmy Gemmell. Although not marked by the extravagant victories of previous title wins, perhaps reflecting the lack of a prolific forward like Campbell, a ten game unbeaten run from November to February saw the title return to the North East once more.

GEORGE HOLLEY

109 GOALS

315 GAMES

15 YEARS (1904-1919)

Born in Seaham in 1885, George Holley joined Sunderland from Seaham White Star in November 1904. During his 15 years at the club, Holley scored a remarkable 160 goals in 315 games, including a hat-trick at St James' Park in the famous 9-1 win of 1908. He was an integral part of the side which won the league title in 1913, and was Sunderland's leading scorer in six of his seasons at Roker Park.

A tricky inside left, Holley's goal scoring exploits made him a central figure to Sunderland's side, and had his time at the club not been interrupted by the First World War his record would almost certainly have been even more impressive. Only three players, Bobby Gurney, Charlie Buchan and David Halliday, scored more goals than Holley in red and white, and Holley can rightly be regarded as one of the greatest players ever to play for the club.

The 1904 illegal Payments scandal

The maximum wage was a great levelling influence on football, but a hugely frustrating one for bigger teams who couldn't take advantage of their greater financial clout. Sunderland were to fall foul of this urge when they found themselves embroiled in a scandal concerning payments made to Scottish international Andrew McCombie. The board of directors gave McCombie £100 (around £6,000 today) to start a business, on the understanding that it was a loan which was to be paid back when McCombie played a benefit game.

McCombie, however, saw the money as a gift, and refused to repay it. Unfortunately for Sunderland, the Football Association saw it the same way, and on looking into Sunderland's records they discovered further discrepancies. Sunderland was fined £250, six directors were suspended for two and a half years, and manager Alex Mackie was suspended for three months. The scandal rocked the club, and brought an end to a period of success under Mackie's stewardship.

GEORGE HOLLEY

109 GOALS

315 GAMES

15 YEARS (1904-1919)

Born in Seaham in 1885, George Holley joined Sunderland from Seaham White Star in November 1904. During his 15 years at the club, Holley scored a remarkable 160 goals in 315 games, including a hat-trick at St James' Park in the famous 9-1 win of 1908. He was an integral part of the side which won the league title in 1913, and was Sunderland's leading scorer in six of his seasons at Roker Park.

A tricky inside left, Holley's goal scoring exploits made him a central figure to Sunderland's side, and had his time at the club not been interrupted by the First World War his record would almost certainly have been even more impressive. Only three players, Bobby Gurney, Charlie Buchan and David Halliday, scored more goals than Holley in red and white, and Holley can rightly be regarded as one of the greatest players ever to play for the club.

The 1904 illegal Payments scandal

The maximum wage was a great levelling influence on football, but a hugely frustrating one for bigger teams who couldn't take advantage of their greater financial clout. Sunderland were to fall foul of this urge when they found themselves embroiled in a scandal concerning payments made to Scottish international Andrew McCombie. The board of directors gave McCombie £100 (around £6,000 today) to start a business, on the understanding that it was a loan which was to be paid back when McCombie played a benefit game.

McCombie, however, saw the money as a gift, and refused to repay it. Unfortunately for Sunderland, the Football Association saw it the same way, and on looking into Sunderland's records they discovered further discrepancies. Sunderland was fined £250, six directors were suspended for two and a half years, and manager Alex Mackie was suspended for three months. The scandal rocked the club, and brought an end to a period of success under Mackie's stewardship.

MANAGERS

Bob Kyle
1905-1928

Born in Belfast, Robert Kyle took the reins at Sunderland in 1905 after Alex Mackie had resigned following the McCombie illegal payments scandal. Kyle was one of 70 applicants for the job of secretary-manager, and would go on to be Sunderland's longest serving manager, with nineteen full seasons of league football under his belt, a record which would have been even more impressive had it not been interrupted by the First World War. He took the club to its first ever FA Cup Final, and won the league championship in 1913.

Kyle oversaw more than 800 Sunderland games, and remains the only Irish manager ever to win the top division of English football. Kyle's career at Sunderland came to an end in 1928 after 23 years at the club, when he retired to be replaced by Johnny Cochrane.

Football League Division One
St James' Park, Newcastle

05/12/1908 / Newcastle United vs Sunderland

Newcastle United /
Lawrence, Whitson, Pudan, Liddell, Veitch, Willis, Duncan, Higgins, Shepherd, Wilson, Gosnell.

Sunderland /
Roose, Forster, Milton, Low, Thompson, Daykin, Mordue, Hogg, Brown, Holley, Bridgett

Newcastle United 1-9 Sunderland
(Hogg hat-trick, Holley hat-trick, Bridgett x2, Mordue, Shepherd)

Sunderland's 9-1 victory away at St James' Park remains the greatest away win in Football League history, and is even more remarkable when you consider the circumstances which surrounded it. Sunderland were sitting mid-table, their attacking flair being counteracted by defensive frailties. Newcastle were on their way to the league title, which they would claim that year for the third time, and were one of the most exciting and attractive teams in England.

The score stood level at the half, Billy Hogg's opener being cancelled out by a Shepherd penalty virtually on the stroke of half time. In the second half, however, the game swung decisively to Sunderland, with 8 goals being scored in 28 minutes, and the visitors actually declaring with 15 minutes to go, sealing a remarkable day for Sunderland.

CHARLIE BUCHAN
Forward
222 Goals
411 Games
13 Years (1911-1924)

One of the most prolific forwards in Sunderland's history, with 222 goals in 411 games for the club Charlie Buchan comes second only to Bobby Gurney in the all time scorer charts. A Londoner, Buchan signed from Leyton in March 1911 and was the club's top scorer every year from 1912-13 until 1924. Instrumental to Sunderland's title win in the 1912-13 season, and central to the side for the next decade, the people of Sunderland were shocked when he was sold to Arsenal in 1925.

Sunderland had demanded £4,000 for Buchan, but Arsenal manager Herbert Chapman ended up striking a bargain at £2,000 plus an extra £100 for every goal he scored during his first year. Buchan scored 21, meaning Arsenal ended up paying £4,100 for his services. His value to the Sunderland team was immeasurable though, and he remains one of the most devastating players ever to pull on a red and white shirt.

No.5 THE 1913 TITLE

The Belfast born Bob Kyle had taken over as Sunderland's secretary-manager from Alex Mackie in 1905, and would remain in charge until 1928, but 1913 was Sunderland's solitary title win under his stewardship. 1913 was a year of ups and downs for the club, reaching their first FA Cup final only to lose at the hands of Aston Villa, however in the league it was Sunderland who got the better of their midlands rivals, beating Villa into second place with 54 points to their 50.

By this time the First Division had begun to look far more recognisable to modern eyes, with 20 teams including Sunderland, Newcastle, Manchester United and City, Everton, Liverpool, Tottenham Hotspur and a Woolwich Arsenal side who were relegated, finishing bottom of the league with just 18 points. The victorious Sunderland team, however, is widely regarded as one of the greatest title winning sides of all time, and probably the greatest Sunderland team ever, with players such as Charlie Buchan, George Holley, Jackie Mordue combining to create a side which won 25 of their 38 games, and restricted defeats to single figures.

FA Cup Final Crystal Palace, London

19/04/1913 / Aston Villa vs Sunderland

Aston Villa /
Hardy, Lyons, Weston, Barber, Harrop, Leach, Wallace, Stephenson, Hampton, Halse, Bache.

Sunderland /
Butler, Gladwin, Ness, Cuggy, Thomson, Low, Mordue, Buchan, Richardson, Holley, Martin.

Aston Villa 1-0 Sunderland
(Barber, 78)

Sunderland's first FA Cup final ended in defeat when, on their way to being league champions, Sunderland saw a landmark double denied by Tommy Barber's late goal. A crowd of 121,919, the second highest in the history of the FA Cup behind the famous 'White Horse' final of 1923, witnessed a bad tempered affair which resulted in Sunderland's invitation to participate in the 1913 Charity Shield being withdrawn, and the referee was subsequently suspended for allowing 17 minutes of stoppage time to be played. It marked the end of Sunderland's first great period, and it would be more than 20 years before they were back in the Cup Final once more.

DAVID HALLIDAY

162 GOALS

175 GAMES

4 YEARS (1925-1929)

Signed for £4,000 in 1925, as a replacement for Charlie Buchan, Scottish forward David Halliday is one of the most prolific forwards in the club's history. In his four years at Sunderland Halliday was top scorer every season, at a time when the club were also blessed with the not inconsiderable attacking talents of Bobby Gurney.

With 162 goals in 175 games, Halliday has the best goals to games ratio of any forward ever to play for Sunderland, an incredible record which he continued during subsequent spells with Arsenal, Manchester City and Clapham Orient. Halliday notched up 12 hat tricks and 3 fours in his time at Sunderland, firing the club to third place finishes in 1926 and 1927 before departing for Arsenal in 1929.

BOBBY GURNEY
228 Goals
390 Games
22 Years (1926-1948)

When Charlie Buchan left for Arsenal in 1925, it was a body blow to many Sunderland fans. Over the preceding 12 years Buchan had been the most prolific player to play for the club, and many people must have been hugely concerned at how they would cope with the loss of their star striker. Fortunately, Sunderland had an ace up their sleeve, a player recommended by Buchan himself after he'd seen him playing for Bishop Auckland.

Silksworth-born Bobby Gurney scored on his debut in April 1926, and would go on to be Sunderland's record goal scorer, with a remarkable 228 goals in 390 games for the club during the next 22 years, a total made more impressive when one takes into account the six years that football was suspended during the Second World War. Buchan had certainly spotted a gem, and Gurney was instrumental in Sunderland's 1936 title and 1937 FA Cup wins, and scoring 10 hat tricks, 2 fours and a five along the way.

MANAGERS

Johnny Cochrane
1928-1939

Born in Paisley, Johnny Cochrane arrived at Sunderland from St Mirren in 1928, as a replacement for Bob Kyle. Although Cochrane couldn't match Kyle's length of service, he was set to become the most successful Sunderland manager of the twentieth century, winning a league title and bringing the FA Cup back to Wearside for the first time. Cochrane was in charge for 500 games between 1928 and 1939, a period which saw players such as Raich Carter, Bobby Gurney and Johnny Mapson appear for the club.

Cochrane was the last Sunderland manager to win a trophy before the Second World War, when he masterminded the FA Cup win of 1937. The title win of 1936 was the last of Sunderland's six, equalling Aston Villa's record, and with that Sunderland became the last team wearing stripes to win the English league title, a record which stands to this day.

RAICH CARTER
Inside Forward
128 Goals
278 Games
8 Years (1931-1939)

Born in Hendon on December 21, 1913, Horatio Stratton Carter would grow up to be one of the finest footballers ever produced in Sunderland, and indeed one of the most naturally talented players ever born in England. A left footed inside forward, although he was equally comfortable with his right, Raich appeared to have an almost mystical understanding of the game, his spectacular ball control and rocket of a shot, with either foot, making him a formidable asset to the Sunderland side for which he made his debut in 1931.

He made 278 appearances for the club, scoring 128 goals, and leading the side to a title win in 1936 and an FA Cup Final victory over Preston North End in 1937. Although his career was interrupted by the Second World War, he moved to Derby County for a fee of £8,000 when hostilities came to an end in 1945. With Derby he won the FA Cup for a second time, making him the only player to win the FA Cup before and after the war. His career concluded with a player-manager role at Hull, and managerial spells at Leeds, Mansfield and Middlesbrough, but he will always be remembered as one of Sunderland's greatest players.

Jimmy Thorpe
1930-1936

On February 5, 1936, Sunderland was struck by tragedy. 22 year old goalkeeper Jimmy Thorpe, kicked in the head and chest during a game against Chelsea at Roker Park four days previously, died of heart failure in hospital from injuries sustained during the match. Sunderland needed a goalkeeper, and needed one badly. The man they chose had played just two games for Third Division Reading, but would prove to be one of the most astute signings the club has ever made.

Johnny Mapson
1936-1954

The 18 year old Johnny Mapson arrived from Reading for £1,500, and would go on to make 383 appearances between the sticks for Sunderland, helping the team to the title in his first year and to their first ever FA Cup win in his second. Although he played for Reading as a guest during the Second World War, he turned down all offers to leave Sunderland, including one from Matt Busby at Manchester United, remaining at the club until his retirement in 1954.

Stats: Player: Mapson. **Position:** Goalkeeper. Years: 18. Games: 383.

No.6 — THE 1936 TITLE

Sunderland's last league title of the twentieth century came in the 1935-36 season, with manager Johnny Cochrane leading his team to an eight point victory over their nearest rivals Derby County. His team was renowned for their goal scoring verve, with club record scorer Bobby Gurney and star inside forward Raich Carter providing formidable firepower which saw them score 109 goals in 42 games. Carter and Gurney were joint top scorers that season, with 31 goals each, in one of the most electric forward lines ever to grace the Roker Park turf. In addition, the season was punctuated with a number of emphatic victories, including three 7-2 score lines, against Bolton and Brentford at Roker Park, and away at Birmingham City.

The 1937 FA Cup Run

16/01/1937 / **FA Cup 3rd Round**
Southampton 2-3 Sunderland (Gurney, Gallacher, Hornby)

30/01/1937 / **FA Cup 4th Round**
Luton Town 2-2 Sunderland (Connor, Duns)

03/02/1937 / **FA Cup 4th Round Replay**
Sunderland 3-1 Luton Town (Duns, Connor, Carter)

20/02/1937 / **FA Cup 5th Round**
Sunderland 3-0 Swansea Town (Duns, Gurney, Caldwell o.g.)

06/03/1937 / **FA Cup 6th Round**
Wolverhampton Wanderers 1-1 Sunderland (Duns)

10/03/1937 / **FA Cup 6th Round Replay**
Sunderland 2-2 Wolverhampton Wanderers (Gurney, Duns)

15/03/1937 / **FA Cup 6th Round Replay (Hillsborough, Sheffield)**
Sunderland 4-0 Wolverhampton Wanderers (Gurney, Carter, Gallacher, Thomson)

10/04/1937 / **FA Cup Semi Final (Leeds Road, Huddersfield)**
Sunderland 2-1 Millwall (Gurney, Gallacher)

FA Cup Final Wembley Stadium, London

01/05/1937 / Sunderland vs Preston North End

Sunderland /
Mapson, Gorman, Hall, Thomson, Johnston, McNab, Duns, Carter, Gurney, Gallacher, Burbanks.

Preston North End /
Burns, Gallimore, Beattie, Shankly, Tremelling, Milne, Dougal, Beresford, F. O'Donnell, Fagan, H. O'Donnell.

Sunderland 3-1 Preston North End
(F. O'Donnell, 44, Gurney, 52, Carter, 72, Burbanks, 85)

Captained by talismanic inside forward Raich Carter, the previous year's league champions came from a goal behind to seal an emphatic win against Preston, and give the Wearsiders their first ever FA Cup. Whilst their league form had been indifferent, seeing them finish 8th in the First Division, they claimed the FA Cup for the first time in their second final and, unbeknownst to them, what was to be their last trophy for almost 40 years.

LEN SHACKLETON

'Clown Prince of Football'
100 Goals
348 Games
9 Years (1948-1957)

The 'Clown Prince of Football', Len Shackleton was born in Bradford on May 3, 1922. Beginning his career at Bradford Park Avenue, he moved to the North East of England in 1946 for £13,000, to play for Newcastle United. He spent two years at St James' Park, but they didn't like his individualistic style, and he was transferred to Sunderland in 1948 for a record sum exceeding £20,000.

He was adored at Sunderland, spending 9 years at Roker Park, during which time he made 348 appearances and scored 100 goals. He was renowned for his dribbling, passing, and shooting, but best loved for his tricks and jokes which included playing one-twos with the corner flag, sitting on the ball to taunt opposition defenders, and once, when 2-1 up against Arsenal, dribbling the ball into the penalty area before putting his foot on it and pretending to comb his hair whilst looking at his watch. Although considered unsportsmanlike by some, and greatly responsible for his regular exclusion from the England squad, it was behaviour like this which endeared him to the Roker faithful and made him a genuine Sunderland legend.

The Bank of England club

It could have been an era of great success; it was certainly an era which promised a great deal to Sunderland fans. Unfortunately, however, it was a promise which was to go unfulfilled. During the early 1950s, Sunderland became known as the 'Bank of England Club', as money was thrown around in a failed attempt to buy success. Signings included a world record transfer of Trevor Ford from Aston Villa for £30,000, who lined up alongside Ivor Broadis (£18,000) and Len Shackleton (£20,500), a star forward line which should have spelled success.

The story of the Bank of England era is more one of frustration than fulfilment, however, as despite star signings, large crowds, and football which was the envy of much of the country, the trophies didn't come. In fact, the only time silverware came back to the North East during that decade was when the FA Cup came to St James' Park three times. The Bank of England Club era came to an end with the illegal payments scandal of 1957, and will always be remembered as one of the greatest false dawns in Sunderland history.

Stan Anderson

A cultured wing half, Stan Anderson remains the only player to captain Sunderland, Newcastle and Middlesbrough. Born in Horden on February 27, 1933, and making his Sunderland debut in 1952, Anderson was one of the local elements of the 'Bank of England' side of the 1950s, turning out for the Roker Park side a grand total of 447 times, notching 35 goals along the way.

Anderson left Sunderland in 1963, crossing the north east's footballing Rubicon when he signed for Newcastle United. He followed that with a move to Middlesbrough in 1965, and succeeded Sunderland icon Raich Carter as Middlesbrough manager in 1966 following his retirement from playing. He also managed AEK Athens, QPR, Doncaster Rovers and Bolton Wanderers before retiring from the game in 1981.

LEN ASHURST

4 GOALS

458 GAMES

12 YEARS (1959-1971)

Left sided defender Len Ashurst holds Sunderland's record for appearances by an outfield player, having turned out for Sunderland a total of 458 times in 12 years at Roker Park. Although he only scored four goals in his time at the club, it's his defensive qualities which are remembered by most, forming part of one of the most settled back fives in the club's history. During his time at Sunderland he saw the rise and fall of the 'Bank of England Club' era, as well as the club's first relegation during the 1957-58 season, and was central to the side which got back into Division One in 1964.

Ashurst left Sunderland to join Hartlepool in 1971, returning to the club as manager in 1984. Although he led the club to its first League Cup final, his side were relegated from the First Division that season and he was sacked in May 1985.

The illegal payments scandal of 1957

In 1957, the maximum wage for a football player in England was £15 a week. In January 1957, a 'Mr Smith' wrote to the Football Association alleging that Sunderland had been circumventing these regulations by making 'under the counter' payments to players. Sunderland had put £3,000 on that year's accounts for straw to cover the pitch, vastly outstripping what was actually required. When the suppliers delivered the straw, they also gave Sunderland credit notes for the amounts returned, and these credit notes were cashed in, with the cash being used to supplement the players' incomes.

Investigations showed that almost five and a half thousand pounds had been given to the players over the preceding half decade using this technique, and Sunderland were punished, with the Chairman and three directors suspended from the game. The club were fined £5,000, the manager Bill Murray was personally fined £200, and resigned at the end of the season. The era of the 'Bank of England Club', which had created so much optimism amongst Sunderland fans, ended in acrimony and disgrace. Injury was added to insult the following year as the club was relegated for the first time.

LEN ASHURST

4 GOALS

458 GAMES

12 YEARS (1959-1971)

Left sided defender Len Ashurst holds Sunderland's record for appearances by an outfield player, having turned out for Sunderland a total of 458 times in 12 years at Roker Park. Although he only scored four goals in his time at the club, it's his defensive qualities which are remembered by most, forming part of one of the most settled back fives in the club's history. During his time at Sunderland he saw the rise and fall of the 'Bank of England Club' era, as well as the club's first relegation during the 1957-58 season, and was central to the side which got back into Division One in 1964.

Ashurst left Sunderland to join Hartlepool in 1971, returning to the club as manager in 1984. Although he led the club to its first League Cup final, his side were relegated from the First Division that season and he was sacked in May 1985.

The illegal payments scandal of 1957

In 1957, the maximum wage for a football player in England was £15 a week. In January 1957, a 'Mr Smith' wrote to the Football Association alleging that Sunderland had been circumventing these regulations by making 'under the counter' payments to players. Sunderland had put £3,000 on that year's accounts for straw to cover the pitch, vastly outstripping what was actually required. When the suppliers delivered the straw, they also gave Sunderland credit notes for the amounts returned, and these credit notes were cashed in, with the cash being used to supplement the players' incomes.

Investigations showed that almost five and a half thousand pounds had been given to the players over the preceding half decade using this technique, and Sunderland were punished, with the Chairman and three directors suspended from the game. The club were fined £5,000, the manager Bill Murray was personally fined £200, and resigned at the end of the season. The era of the 'Bank of England Club', which had created so much optimism amongst Sunderland fans, ended in acrimony and disgrace. Injury was added to insult the following year as the club was relegated for the first time.

Charlie Hurley - 'King' Charlie
1957-1969

The greatest hero ever to play in red and white. Known for his classy defending and his powerful headed goals

It's often the centre forwards who make themselves the heroes, but for many people the greatest hero ever to play in red and white wasn't a centre forward but a centre back. Charlie Hurley was born in Cork on October 4, 1936, moving to Essex with his family when he was just seven months old. He began his career at Millwall, moving to Sunderland in September 1957. His career got off to an inauspicious start, with a 7-0 defeat against Blackpool and an own goal on his debut, but fortunately for all concerned things could only get better, and Charlie spent the next 12 years at the club. Known for his classy defending and his powerful headed goals, 'King' Charlie racked up 401 appearances and 26 goals for Sunderland, and wrote himself into the history of the club.

Stats: Position: Centre Back. Years: 12. Games: 401. Goals: 26.

JIMMY MONTGOMERY

GOALKEEPER

627 GAMES ★ ★ ★ ★ ★ ★ ★ ★ ★ ★ ★ ★ ★ ★ ★

15 YEARS (1961-1976)

Born in Hendon in 1943, and central to the club's greatest moment since the Second World War, Jimmy Montgomery is the all time record appearance maker for his hometown club. Montgomery made his debut as a 17 year old in 1961, and played his final game for Sunderland in a League Cup match against Manchester United in 1976.

Between those two points he played 627 times, had four ever-present seasons, and of course pulled off what many describe as the best save in Wembley history when he denied Trevor Cherry and Peter Lorimer in the 1973 FA Cup Final. Montgomery finished his playing days at Southampton, Birmingham City and Nottingham Forest where he got a European Cup winner's medal as an unused sub in the 1980 final.

Brian Clough
1961-1964

He will always be the best striker they ever saw play and the best manager Sunderland never had

He may be known to the football world as a manager, but it's his exploits as a goal-scorer which keeps Brian Clough close to the hearts of Sunderland supporters. Scoring 63 goals in 74 games for the club between 1961 and 1964, Clough is one of the most prolific forwards ever to play for Sunderland, his career cut tragically short by a cruciate ligament injury sustained against Bury on Boxing Day 1962.

His record at Sunderland is made all the more remarkable by the fact that the overwhelming majority of his goals for the club came before his injury, managing just three games on his return before he was forced to retire from football altogether. His record following this is a matter of record, with league titles, cup wins, and of course back to back European Cups with Nottingham Forest making him a well known and well respected figure in football. However, for many Sunderland fans he will always be the best striker they ever saw play and the best manager Sunderland never had.

Stats: Position: Forward. Years: 3. Games: 74. Goals: 63.

BOBBY KERR

'The Little General'

6 Years (1973-1979)

At only 5'5" in his stockinged feet, one might think that Bobby Kerr's diminutive stature would preclude him from a role as a midfield enforcer, but 'the little general', as he was known, can justifiably claim to be one of Sunderland's most inspirational captains. Having twice broken his leg at the start of his Sunderland career, many must have feared for Bobby's future at the club, but he overcame such challenges to lead Sunderland to their greatest post-war success. In doing so, he became the shortest captain ever to lift the FA Cup, a record which still stands to this day.

Following the triumph in 1973, Kerr remained at Sunderland for the following 6 years, leading the club to promotion in 1976, before departing Sunderland in March 1979 to play for Blackpool and his old boss, Bob Stokoe.

The Vancouver Royal Canadians

In 1967, following the great success of the 1966 World Cup, the North American Soccer League (NASL) was set up in the United States. It had originally been intended to start in 1968, but when a rival league, the National Professional Soccer League (NPSL) was set up, NASL changed its name to the United Soccer Association and brought its start date forward a year to 1967. This meant that there wasn't enough time to assemble teams in the usual way, so foreign teams were imported wholesale and placed in US and Canadian cities. One such team was Sunderland.

Sunderland became the Vancouver Royal Canadians for the duration of the summer league, and it was to be their only season in the USA, with a disappointing return of 3 wins, 4 losses and 5 draws from the 12 games played. From 1968 the USA merged with the NPSL, taking the North American Soccer League name, and although the Vancouver Royal Canadians played once more it was without Sunderland's involvement, with players from across the globe coached by the legendary Hungarian Ferenc Puskas.

GARY ROWELL

103 GOALS

297 GAMES

12 YEARS (1972-1984)

Born in Seaham on June 6, 1957, Gary Rowell is that rarest of beasts, a genuine, home-grown, Sunderland hero. Scoring 103 goals in his 297 games for the club, Rowell's record makes him Sunderland's second highest post-war goal scorer, with only Kevin Phillips having notched more goals for the club. Joining as a youth player in 1972, Rowell will be remembered by many fans for his hat-trick in the 1979 derby at St James' Park, but he was also Sunderland's top scorer every season from 1977-78 to 1983-84.

His career was beset by injuries, however, after being injured in a game against Leyton Orient in March 1979. He left the club in 1984 as part of Len Ashurst's remodelling of the Sunderland side, moving to Norwich City, but he sustained a serious injury in his first pre-season. He finished his career at Middlesbrough, Brighton, Dundee, Carlisle and Burnley, retiring in 1990.

MANAGERS

Bob Stokoe
1972-1987

Born September 21, 1930 in Mickley, Northumberland, Bob Stokoe is one of the rare people to be loved on both sides of the north east's footballing divide. Starting his career at Newcastle in 1946, Stokoe grew into a tough tackling centre half, making his debut against Middlesbrough in 1950 and remaining at the club for the next ten years, including an appearance in the 1955 FA Cup victory over Manchester City.

On Wearside, however, Stokoe is far more fondly remembered for his managerial achievements.

Taking over at Roker Park in November 1972, with the club sitting fourth bottom of the Second Division, Stokoe masterminded a remarkable turnaround which not only saw the club achieve safety by the end of the season, but achieve one of the great underdog victories of all time, beating Leeds United 1-0 to win the 1973 FA Cup. Stokoe also led the club to promotion in the 1975-76 season, but retired the following October. He returned in 1987 in a failed attempt to save the club from relegation to the Third Division, retiring from football at the end of that season.

The 1973 FA Cup Run

13/01/1973 / **FA Cup 3rd Round**
Notts County 1-1 Sunderland (Bradd, Watson)

16/01/1973 / **FA Cup 3rd Round Replay**
Sunderland 2-0 Notts County (Watson, Tueart)

03/02/1973 / **FA Cup 4th Round**
Sunderland 1-1 Reading (Chappell, Tueart)

07/02/1973 / **FA Cup 4th Round Replay**
Reading 1-3 Sunderland (Watson, Tueart, Kerr, Cumming)

24/02/1973 / **FA Cup 5th Round**
Manchester City 2-2 Sunderland (Towers, Horswill, Hughes, Montgomery o.g.)

27/02/1973 / **FA Cup 5th Round Replay**
Sunderland 3-1 Manchester City (Halom, Hughes, Lee, Hughes)

17/03/1973 / **FA Cup 6th Round**
Sunderland 2-0 Luton Town (Watson, Guthrie)

17/04/1973 / **FA Cup Semi Final (Hillsborough, Sheffield)**
Arsenal 1-2 Sunderland (Halom, Hughes, George)

MANAGERS

Bob Stokoe
1972-1987

Born September 21, 1930 in Mickley, Northumberland, Bob Stokoe is one of the rare people to be loved on both sides of the north east's footballing divide. Starting his career at Newcastle in 1946, Stokoe grew into a tough tackling centre half, making his debut against Middlesbrough in 1950 and remaining at the club for the next ten years, including an appearance in the 1955 FA Cup victory over Manchester City.

On Wearside, however, Stokoe is far more fondly remembered for his managerial achievements.

Taking over at Roker Park in November 1972, with the club sitting fourth bottom of the Second Division, Stokoe masterminded a remarkable turnaround which not only saw the club achieve safety by the end of the season, but achieve one of the great underdog victories of all time, beating Leeds United 1-0 to win the 1973 FA Cup. Stokoe also led the club to promotion in the 1975-76 season, but retired the following October. He returned in 1987 in a failed attempt to save the club from relegation to the Third Division, retiring from football at the end of that season.

The 1973 FA Cup Run

13/01/1973 / **FA Cup 3rd Round**
Notts County 1-1 Sunderland (Bradd, Watson)

16/01/1973 / **FA Cup 3rd Round Replay**
Sunderland 2-0 Notts County (Watson, Tueart)

03/02/1973 / **FA Cup 4th Round**
Sunderland 1-1 Reading (Chappell, Tueart)

07/02/1973 / **FA Cup 4th Round Replay**
Reading 1-3 Sunderland (Watson, Tueart, Kerr, Cumming)

24/02/1973 / **FA Cup 5th Round**
Manchester City 2-2 Sunderland (Towers, Horswill, Hughes, Montgomery o.g.)

27/02/1973 / **FA Cup 5th Round Replay**
Sunderland 3-1 Manchester City (Halom, Hughes, Lee, Hughes)

17/03/1973 / **FA Cup 6th Round**
Sunderland 2-0 Luton Town (Watson, Guthrie)

17/04/1973 / **FA Cup Semi Final (Hillsborough, Sheffield)**
Arsenal 1-2 Sunderland (Halom, Hughes, George)

FA Cup Final Wembley Stadium, London

05/05/1973 / Leeds United vs Sunderland

Leeds United /
Harvey, Reaney, Cherry, Bremner, Madeley, Hunter, Lorimer, Clarke, Jones, Giles, Gray. Sub: Yorath.

Sunderland /
Montgomery, Malone, Guthrie, Horswill, Watson, Pitt, Kerr, Hughes, Halom, Porterfield, Tueart. Sub: Young.

Leeds United 0-1 Sunderland
(Porterfield, 31)

A victory for the underdog, remembered by many as one of the most surprising FA Cup Final results of all time. The goal may have been scored by Ian Porterfield, but the headlines would go to the incredible acrobatics of Jimmy Montgomery's second half double save from Cherry and Lorimer, and the Cup would make its way back to Sunderland for the first time since 1937.

Football League Division Two
St James' Park, Newcastle

24/02/1979 / Newcastle United vs Sunderland

Newcastle United /
Hardwick, Brownlie, Nattrass, Martin, Bird, Blackley, Shoulder, Walker, Withe, Hibbitt, Connolly. Sub: Mitchell (Blackley, 45).

Sunderland /
Siddall, Henderson, Bolton, Arnott, Clarke, Elliott, Chisholm, Rostron, Entwhistle, Lee, Rowell. Sub: Doherty (Arnott, 75).

Newcastle United 1-4 Sunderland
(Rowell, 6, Rowell, 25, Connolly, 50, Rowell, 62, Entwhistle, 71).

Seaham-born Gary Rowell wrote himself into history in February 1979 with a stunning hat-trick to condemn Newcastle United to defeat on home turf. The victory saw Sunderland climb fifth top of the Second Division, with Newcastle dropping to eighth from bottom. Sunderland were to finish the season fourth, just one point from promotion, whilst Newcastle ended the year 13 points behind in eighth, but it is for that day in February, that 1979 will be remembered by Sunderland fans, especially by those lucky enough to be at St James' Park.

GARY BENNETT

25 GOALS

443 GAMES

11 YEARS (1984-1995)

The Manchester born defender Gary Bennett joined Sunderland from Cardiff in July 1984, for a fee of £85,000. After scoring just two minutes into his debut, Bennett went on to appear 443 times in his 11 years at the club, scoring 25 goals. He played for Sunderland at Wembley four times, the 1985 League Cup Final, 1988 League Centenary Tournament, 1990 Playoff final and 1992 FA Cup final.

A tough tackling defender, Bennett was at the club through a turbulent period, being part of 3 relegations, 2 promotions, and two cup finals. He won the player of the year award twice, in 1987 and 1994, and will be remembered for his adventurous play and his committed record as the club's captain.

Football League Cup Final
Wembley Stadium, London

24/03/1985 / Norwich City vs Sunderland

Norwich City /
Woods, Haylock, van Wijk, Bruce, Mendham, Waton, Barham, Channon, Deehan, Hartford, Donowa. Sub: Devine.

Sunderland /
Turner, Venison, Pickering, Bennett, Chisholm, Corner, Daniel, Wallace, Hodgson, Berry, Walker. Sub: Gayle (Corner).

Norwich City 1-0 Sunderland
(Chisholm o.g.)

Sunderland's first League Cup final ended in a defeat at the hands of Norwich as the trophy made its way back to East Anglia rather than to Wearside. An own goal by Gordon Chisholm following a mistake by David Corner whilst attempting to see a ball out for a goal kick, rather than clear it into touch, as well as a second half penalty miss by Clive Walker, meant that this was an altogether unpleasant day for Sunderland's travelling fans.

Marco Gabbiadini

Half of the famous 'G-Force', along with Eric Gates, Marco Gabbiadini joined newly relegated Sunderland from York City in the summer of 1987, following his manager Denis Smith into Roker Park. Smith saw Gabbiadini as the man Sunderland needed to fire them out of the Third Division, and so it proved, with the £80,000 outlay on the 19 year old Marco looking like some of the best money the club had ever spent.

Marco scored 21 goals in 31 games that season, the club took the Third Division title, and Marco made himself a hero for a whole generation of Sunderland fans. He was instrumental in the club being promoted once more, and remained a Sunderland player until relegation at the end of the 1990-91 season saw him leave to ply his trade at Crystal Palace, Derby County, and six other clubs, finally retiring a Hartlepool player in January 2004.

Second Division Playoff Final
Wembley Stadium, London

28/05/1990 / Swindon Town vs Sunderland

Swindon Town /
Digby, Kerslake, Bodin, McLoughlin, Calderwood, Gittens, Jones, Shearer, White, MacLaren, Foley. Subs: Hockaday, Simpson

Sunderland /
Norman, Kay, Agboola, Bennett, MacPhail, Owers, Bracewell, Armstrong, Gates, Gabbiadini, Pascoe. Subs: Hauser (Gates, 72), Atkinson (Pascoe, 69).

Swindon Town 1-0 Sunderland
(McLoughlin, 26)

After a famous 2-0 victory at St James' Park in the second leg of the semi final, Sunderland went down 1-0 to a speculative Alan McLoughlin effort from 30 yards which took a wicked deflection off Gary Bennett to loop over Tony Norman and into the back of the net. Swindon celebrated promotion, and Sunderland fans resigned themselves to another year in the Second Division. Ten days later, however, Swindon were found guilty of making illegal payments to players and denied promotion, with Sunderland being elevated to the First Division in their stead.

KEVIN BALL

Central Defender. Midfield.

388 Games

9 Years (1990-1999)

Having made 388 appearances in his nine years as a Sunderland player, and spent seven of those nine years as captain, Hastings born Kevin Ball can justifiably claim to be an adopted Wearsider. Joining from Portsmouth for £350,000 in July 1990, Ball quickly endeared himself to the Roker faithful. Known for his uncompromising style, Ball started his time at Sunderland as a central defender, moving into midfield as his career progressed. He was instrumental in leading the club to promotion in 1996 and again in 1999, as well as representing the club at Wembley on two occasions, the 1992 FA Cup final and the 1998 Playoff final.

Leaving Sunderland for Fulham in December 1999, Ball finally retired from the game whilst playing for Burnley in 2002, returning to Sunderland as a coach. He was caretaker manager of the club for ten games following the departure of Mick McCarthy in 2006, but relinquished his role after his former teammate Niall Quinn's, Drumaville Consortium, successfully took over the club, returning to his position on the backroom staff.

FA Cup Final Wembley Stadium, London

09/05/1992 / Liverpool vs Sunderland

Liverpool /
Grobbelaar, Jones, Burrows, Nicol, Mølby, Wright, Saunders, Houghton, Rush, McManaman, Thomas. Subs: Marsh, Walters.

Sunderland /
Norman, Owers, Ball, Bennett, Rogan, Rush, Bracewell, Davenport, Armstrong, Byrne, Atkinson. Subs: Hardyman (Rush, 69), Hawke (Armstrong, 77).

Liverpool 2-0 Sunderland
(Thomas, 47, Rush, 68)

Sadly, the underdog victory of 1973 was not repeated in 1992, as Second Division Sunderland went down 2-0 to a Liverpool side which had just finished sixth in the First Division under the management of Graeme Souness. Malcolm Crosby's Sunderland side were the first to reach the FA Cup final since 1973, with John Byrne scoring in every round except the final.

Michael Gray

On November 21, 1992, Michael Gray made his Sunderland debut in a match against Derby County at Roker Park. He was only 18 years old at the time, but a goal on his debut was the perfect start to a career which would see him spend more than 10 years at the club, making 410 appearances, and captain of the team on numerous occasions. Over the years he featured on the left and right wings, and even as a striker, but it was the left back position he was to make his own, his overlapping runs causing havoc in the opposition half.

Gray scored Sunderland's first Premier League goal, against Nottingham Forest in 1996, although he may well be better remembered for the goal he didn't score, the missed penalty in the 1998 playoff final. He was a vital part of Peter Reid's title-winning side the following season, and remained at the club until 2003 when he moved on, first to Celtic on loan and then to Blackburn Rovers, Leeds, Wolves, ending his career at Sheffield Wednesday in 2010.

Niall Quinn
1996-2012

Probably the best signing Reid ever made

Kevin Phillips' goal scoring exploits in Peter Reid's side may have written him into the Sunderland history books, but for many it is his strike partner who remains the true Sunderland icon. Born in Dublin on October 6, 1966, Niall John Quinn moved to Arsenal in 1983, scoring on his debut against Liverpool. After losing his place at Arsenal to Alan Smith, he moved to Manchester City in 1990, and was brought to Sunderland by Peter Reid in 1996 for a club record, £1.3m.

Quinn was Reid's marquee signing, but his first season was beset by injuries and many feared that he would turn out to be a waste of money. In fact, he was probably the best signing Reid ever made. An essential part of Reid's team, creating for Kevin Phillips, while scoring numerous goals of his own, Quinn enjoyed a resurgence in his career at Sunderland, finally retiring in 2003.

His greatest contribution to the club was to come, however, when he returned in 2006 to head the Drumaville Consortium, buying the club from Bob Murray and bringing in first Roy Keane, then Steve Bruce, and finally Martin O'Neill, whilst also managing the transition from Drumaville's ownership to that of Ellis Short. Quinn left Sunderland in 2012, but remains a true hero of the club.

Stats: Position: Striker. Years: 7. **Position:** Chairman. Years: 6.

KEVIN PHILLIPS

115 GOALS

209 GAMES

6 YEARS (1997-2003)

When Peter Reid paid Watford £350,000 for Kevin Phillips in 1997, nobody could have predicted just quite how devastating the little man from Hertfordshire would turn out to be. Born on July 25, 1973, Phillips was a youth player at Southampton, before moving to Baldock Town and then Watford, where Reid spotted his talents.

His first season at Sunderland was a whirlwind, scoring on his debut against Manchester City and racking up 35 league goals in all competitions as Sunderland lost out to Charlton in a heartbreaking Wembley playoff defeat. The next two seasons saw him bang in 25 during an injury hit season in the First Division, followed by a record breaking 30 goals in the Premier League, winning him the European Golden Boot in the process. In total, during his six seasons at the club Phillips scored 115 goals in 209 games, making him Sunderland's record post-war goal scorer and the most prolific centre forward in red and white since Brian Clough.

The Stadium of Light
1997-Present

Opening in July 1997, and built on the site of the former Wearmouth Colliery, the Stadium of Light has been Sunderland's permanent home since the club was forced to leave Roker Park. Following the introduction of all-seater stadia by the Taylor Report, Roker Park was judged too small, and the surrounding area too built up to allow the club to expand. Numerous options were explored as alternatives to the club's home since 1898, with land next to the Nissan car plant emerging as the frontrunner. However, and some would say fortunately, the plans to build at Nissan did not come to fruition, and an alternative site on the north bank of the river Wear was chosen.

Although planning permission was originally given for a 34,000 seat stadium, this rose to 40,000, and finally 42,000 by the time construction was complete. The ground was extended again in 2000 following the heroic exploits of Peter Reid's great side, with the final ground capacity reaching 49,000. The stadium is designed so that the pitch is several meters below ground level, with people entering half way up the lower tier, meaning that the Stadium of Light, almost uniquely for a football stadium, looks bigger on the inside.

First Division Playoff Final
Wembley Stadium, London

25/05/1998 / Charlton Athletic vs Sunderland

Charlton Athletic /
Ilic, Mills, Bowen, Rufus, Youds, Jones, Newton, Kinsella, Heaney, Mendonca, Bright. Subs: Robinson (for Mills, 76), Brown (Bright, 93), Jones (Heaney, 65).

Sunderland /
Perez, Holloway, Gray, Craddock, Williams, Johnston, Clark, Ball, Summerbee, Quinn, Phillips. Subs: Makin (Holloway, 45), Rae (Clark, 100), Dichio (Phillips, 73).

Charlton Athletic 4-4 Sunderland
(Mendonca, 23, Quinn, 50, Phillips, 58, Mendonca, 71, Quinn, 73, Rufus, 85, Summerbee, 99, Mendonca, 103)

Penalties /

Mendonca	✓	Summerbee	✓
Brown	✓	Johnston	✓
Jones	✓	Ball	✓
Kinsella	✓	Makin	✓
Bowen	✓	Rae	✓
Robinson	✓	Quinn	✓
Newton	✓	Gray	✗

FA Cup Semi Final Old Trafford, Manchester

04/04/2004 / Millwall vs Sunderland

Millwall /
Marshall, Lawrence, Muscat, Ward, Livermore, Cahill, Wise, Ifill, Dichio, Ryan, Harris. Subs: Roberts (Muscat, 42), Sweeney (Ifill, 29), Elliott (Ryan, 56), Gueret, Chadwick.

Sunderland /
Poom, McCartney, Babb, Breen, Wright, Arca, Thirlwell, McAteer, Oster, Kyle, Smith. Subs: Myhre, Williams, Piper (Babb, 77), Thornton (Wright, 90), Stewart (Smith, 61).

Millwall 1-0 Sunderland
(Cahill, 26, McAteer sent off, 85)

A crowd of more than 56,000 were at Old Trafford to see Tim Cahill deny Mick McCarthy's Sunderland side a first trip to Wembley since the 1998 Playoff final, and a first FA Cup final since the 1992 defeat by Liverpool. John Oster came closest for Sunderland on 7 minutes when his free kick hit the underside of the bar and bounced out, but it was the side of Tim Cahill's foot which sealed it on 26 minutes and sent another generation of Sunderland fans home thinking about what might have been.

Football League Championship Playoff Second Leg Stadium of Light, Sunderland

17/05/2004 / Sunderland vs Crystal Palace

Sunderland /
Poom, McCartney, Breen, Babb, Bjorklund, Oster, Whitley, McAteer, Thornton, Kyle, Stewart. Subs: Myhre, Clark, Williams (Bjorklund, 105), Robinson (Thornton, 69), Tommy Smith (Stewart, 84).

Crystal Palace /
Vaesen, Granville, Leigertwood, Popovic, Butterfield, Gray, Hughes, Riihilati, Routledge, Shipperley, Johnson. Subs: Berthelin, Black, Powell (Granville, 72), Derry (Riihilati, 58), Freedman (Butterfield, 61).

Sunderland 2-1 Crystal Palace
(4-4 on aggregate) (Kyle, 42, Stewart, 45, Powell, 90, Gray sent off, 85)

Penalties /

Oster	× 0-0	Johnson	✓ 0-1
Smith	✓ 1-1	Freedman	✓ 1-2
Babb	✓ 2-2	Shipperley	✓ 2-3
Robinson	✓ 3-3	Popovic	✓ 3-4
Breen	✓ 4-4	Derry	× 4-4
McAteer	× 4-4	Routledge	× 4-4
Whitley	× 4-4	Hughes	✓ 4-5

Mick McCarthy's first full term on Wearside ended in disappointment as Sunderland lost out on penalties to Crystal Palace, who went on to be promoted. It would take Sunderland another season in the Championship to achieve that feat; McCarthy's team going up as champions the following year.

Football League Championship
Stadium of Light, Sunderland

27/04/2007 / Sunderland vs Burnley

Sunderland /
Ward, Simpson, Nosworthy, Evans, Collins, Edwards, Whitehead, Miller, Stokes, Murphy, Connolly. Subs: Fulop, Leadbitter (Miller, 73), Hysen (Stokes, 71), Yorke, John (Connolly, 86).

Burnley /
Jensen, Duff, Thomas, Caldwell, Harley, Elliott, Djemba-Djemba, McCann, Jones, Gray, McVeigh. Subs: Coyne, Coughlan, Spicer (Elliott, 73), Gudjonsson (McCann, 29), Akinbyi (Jones, 58).

Sunderland 3-2 Burnley
(Murphy, 14, Gray, 39 pen, Elliott, 50, Connolly, 54 pen, Edwards, 80)

Carlos Edwards' screamer sealed a memorable first year on Wearside for Roy Keane, as Sunderland's win over Burnley put them back at the top of the league with one game to play. That Friday night in April epitomised the season, with attacking football from both sides, with fantastic goals, a missed penalty from David Connolly, all serving to confirm that whatever life under Keane's regime would be, it certainly wouldn't be boring. Sunderland headed off to Luton the following week knowing that victory would see them promoted, a victory (and a league title) sealed with five emphatic goals at Kenilworth Road.

FA Premier League
Stadium of Light, Sunderland

25/10/2008 / Sunderland vs Newcastle United

Sunderland /
Fulop, Chimbonda, Ferdinand, Collins, McCartney, Malbranque, Whitehead, Yorke, Richardson, Cisse, Diouf. Subs: Colgan, Bardsley, Tainio (Malbranque, 87), Reid (Diouf, 90), Chopra, Jones (Yorke, 57).

Newcastle United /
Given, Beye, Taylor, Coloccini, Bassong, Geremi, Guthrie, Butt, Duff, Ameobi, Martins. Subs: Harper, Cacapa, Jose Enrique (Bassong, 84), Gutierrez (Geremi, 73), Barton (Butt, 85), N'Zogbia, Xisco.

Sunderland 2-1 Newcastle United
(Cisse, 20, Ameobi, 30, Richardson, 75)

It was the beginning of the end for Roy Keane, but what a beginning. Malbranque's run for Cisse's opener, Ameobi's equaliser threatening to spoil the day, and then Richardson's rocket thundering past Given on 75 minutes. Jones might have made it three, but by the end nobody in red and white was that bothered, as Sunderland celebrated their first derby win on Wearside for 28 years.

Vital Statistics

Most league goals scored in a season
109 in 42 games, 1955-56 (First Division)

Fewest league goals scored in a season
21 in 38 games, 2002-03 (Premier League)

Most league goals conceded in a season
97 in 42 games, 1957-58 (First Division)

Fewest league goals conceded in a season
26 in 34 games, 1900-01 (First Division)

Most points in a season (two points for a win)
61 in 42 games, 1962-63 (First Division)

Most points in a season (three points for a win)
105 in 46 games, 1998-99 (First Division)

Fewest points in a season (two points for a win)
23 in 22 games, 1890-91, and in 30 games, 1896-97 (both First Division)

Fewest points in a season (three points for a win)
15 points in 38 games, 2005-06 (Premier League)

Record league win
Newcastle United 1-9 Sunderland (December 5, 1908)

Record league defeat
8-0 vs Sheffield Wednesday (December 26, 1911)
8-0 vs West Ham United (October 19, 1968)
8-0 vs Watford (September 25, 1982)